Published by Tails and Tales, LLC
Printed by Oswego Printing Company, Inc.
Oswego, New York

ISBN # 978-0-9832626-8-8

Never ride alone!

Charlotte's
Big Dream

by
Connie Evans
Illustrations by
Jim Arnold

DEDICATION

To Tiger Lilly

This book is dedicated not only to Lilly, who has spent over 800 days waiting for a family to call her own, but to all the animals in shelters and rescues waiting for someone to see how special they truly are. Please share this book so perhaps someone will see Tiger Lilly and decide she is the perfect dog for them. Save a life adopt a shelter pet.

Please help me find
my forever family.
Love,
Tiger Lilly

Dear Reader,

The inspiration for each of these cartoons is pulled from my daily life with an eclectic crew of dogs and cats. Everyday they make me smile, laugh and cry. I sometimes just sit and scratch my head at their, as my Grandmother would say, shenanigans.

The sale of this book and all the books in the Reading For Rescue Series goes directly to help homeless animals in our community.

Thank you for making a difference in the life of a furry friend. Enjoy!

Connie Evans

BEST
FRIENDS

To you they are "just dogs"
To me they are family

Free hugs given daily

IT'S
ALL
ABOUT
LOVE

Bad hair day

Ever feel like you're being watched?

Dog Dreams

More Dog Dreams

I am beautiful inside and out.

TEACHING
and
LEARNING

Wisdom from older sister Annie

Rule 1: never pick a fight with a cat.

Just because it's black and white doesn't mean it's a kitty.

Just because the cat buried it doesn't make it treasure

Charlotte tells a ~~tail~~ tale

If pit bulls were superheroes
their super strength would be
the ability to melt your heart with a single glance

ID tags save lives!

Don't leave your best friend out in the cold.

Dream Big

ADVICE FROM A DOG

Advice from a dog:

Always accessorize

Advice from a dog:

Always live in the moment

Advice from a dog:

Always ride with the top down.

Advice from a dog:

Life's a ball

Advice from a dog:

Always be kind.

Advice from a dog:

Play with gusto

Advice from a dog:

Life is short,
hug your friends

CELEBRATIONS

Remember: We are not an Easter gift–

We are a ten year commitment!

HAPPY 4th OF JULY!

Charlotte's
Big Dream

JA

The DOG days of summer

Charlotte's
Big Dream

Charlotte's
Big Dream

Giving Thanks

May you be wrapped in warmth and love
this Holiday Season.

Dear Santa,
Please help my friends at
the Animal Shelter
Love,
Charlotte

BE A HERO.
SAVE A LIFE.
ADOPT A SHELTER PET.

BELIEVE

ANGELS WINGS
&
OTHER THINGS

Thank you, VMC

for getting my sister back up on all fours!

We love ya!

Good Dental Health
Important for People and Pets

Sometimes the smallest hands make the biggest difference.

Please remember those less fortunate.

Pet Partners® of Syracuse

Changing lives ... one visit at a time

Forever Faithful

Rainbow Bridge

In loving memory of JoAnne Parker,
Rescuer extraordinaire

ACKNOWLEDGEMENTS

The following animals, people, and organizations are represented in various drawings throughout this book:

My best friends, Charlotte & Sawyer
Dr Ariane Hamblin-Smith, DVM
Dr Barbara Panko, DDS
Veterinary Medical Center (VMC)
Cuse Pit Crew
Katie & Loki
Di Keavney
Renee & Angel
Callie
Akasha
Liam
Summer
Carol & Stuart
Bella
Apollo

Pet Partners of Syracuse

JoAnne Parker